THE SACRAMENT OF RECONCILIATION

MAKING THINGS RIGHT

REVISED

JEANNINE TIMKO LEICHNER

ILLUSTRATED BY KEVIN DAVIDSON

Our Sunday Visitor Publishing Division
Our Sunday Visitor, Inc.
Huntington, Indiana 46750

Nihil Obstat: Rev. Michael Heintz
Censor Librorum

Imprimatur: ✠ John M. D'Arcy
Bishop of Fort Wayne-South Bend
June 27, 2005

The *Nihil Obstat* and *Imprimatur* are official declarations that a book or pamphlet is free from doctrinal or moral error. It is not implied that those who have granted the *Nihil Obstat* and *Imprimatur* agree with the contents, opinions, or statements expressed.

The Scripture citations used in *"Making Things Right*: Parent/Catechist Guide" are taken from the *Catholic Edition of the Revised Standard Version of the Bible* (RSV), copyright © 1965 and 1966 by the Division of Christian Education of the National Council of the Churches of Christ in the United States of America. Used by permission. All rights reserved.

Catechism excerpts are from the English translation of the *Catechism of the Catholic Church, Second Edition,* for use in the United States of America, copyright © 1994 and 1997, United States Catholic Conference — Libreria Editrice Vaticana. Used by permission. All rights reserved.

The Prayer of Absolution (n. 46) and the penance quotation (n. 6) are from the *Rite of Penance,* copyright © 1974 by the International Committee on English in the Liturgy, Inc. (ICEL). Used by permission. All rights reserved.

Every reasonable effort has been made to determine copyright holders of excerpted materials and to secure permissions as needed. If any copyrighted materials have been inadvertently used in this work without proper credit being given in one form or another, please notify Our Sunday Visitor in writing so that future printings of this work may be corrected accordingly.

Our Sunday Visitor Publishing Division
Our Sunday Visitor, Inc.
200 Noll Plaza
Huntington, IN 46750

ISBN: 978-1-59276-157-9 (Inventory No. X208)

Cover design by Rebecca Heaston; cover art by Kevin Davidson
Interior art and design by Kevin Davidson

PRINTED IN THE UNITED STATES OF AMERICA

If you have ever felt alone and sad
because of something you did,
if you have ever wished you
could make things right again,
this little book is for <u>you</u>.

My name is _____.

I am _____ years old.

This is my picture

I like to

___ play games

___ read

___ ride a bike

___ draw

___ sing

___ _____

I am the only person in the world just like me.

GOD LOVES ME!

God loves each of us more than we can ever imagine.

When we were baptized, God filled us with new life and made us part of his own family.

MY BAPTISM

I was baptized on

_____.

I am a child of God!

God's family is called the **CHURCH**.

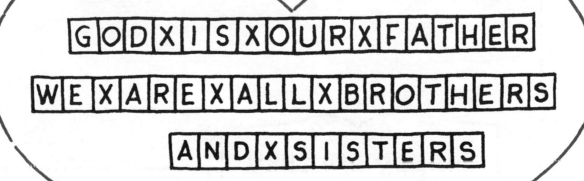

GODXISXOURXFATHER

WEXAREXALLXBROTHERS

ANDXSISTERS

God wants everyone in his family to love him.

He also wants us to love one another and to live together peacefully.

Find or draw a picture of people showing love for each other.

Happy are they who walk in God's ways.

Psalm 119:1

Jesus' heart was full of love for God and for other people.

During his life on earth, Jesus showed his love in many ways.

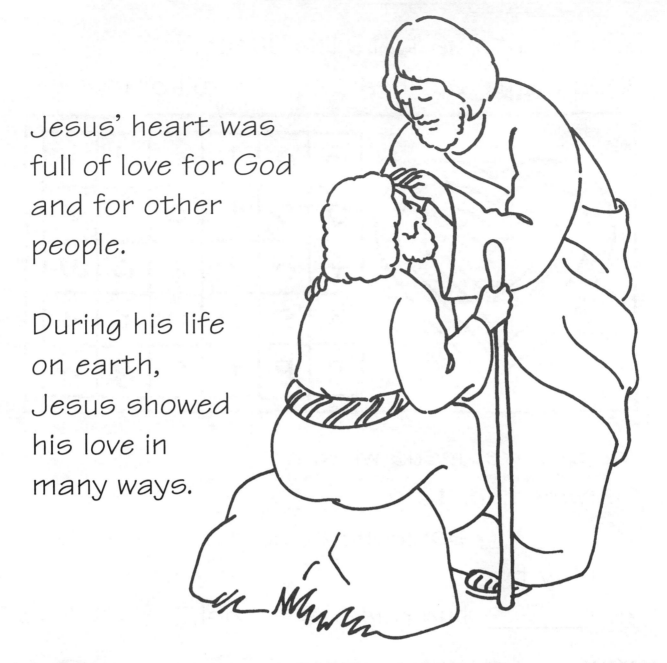

Can you match these?

He made blind people ...	sick people.
He cured ...	see again.
He fed the ...	how to pray.
He taught people ...	hungry crowd.

5

God wants us to be like Jesus.
God wants our hearts to be full of love.

h	e	l	p	d	x
o	s	f	a	i	r
f	o	l	l	o	w
k	s	h	a	r	e
g	p	r	a	y	w

We are like Jesus when we
 1. remember to p_____.
 2. h_____ someone at home.
 3. play f_____.
 4. f_____ the rules at school.
 5. s_____ our toys.

When we love others, we love God!

Think about a time when you were like Jesus.
Draw a picture or write a story about it.

Love is patient.
Love is kind.
Love is not jealous.
1 Corinthians 13:4

7

Have you ever thrown a rock
into some water and watched
the ripples get bigger
and bigger?

Whenever we do something good for
someone, the love ripples through other
people's lives like ripples on water.

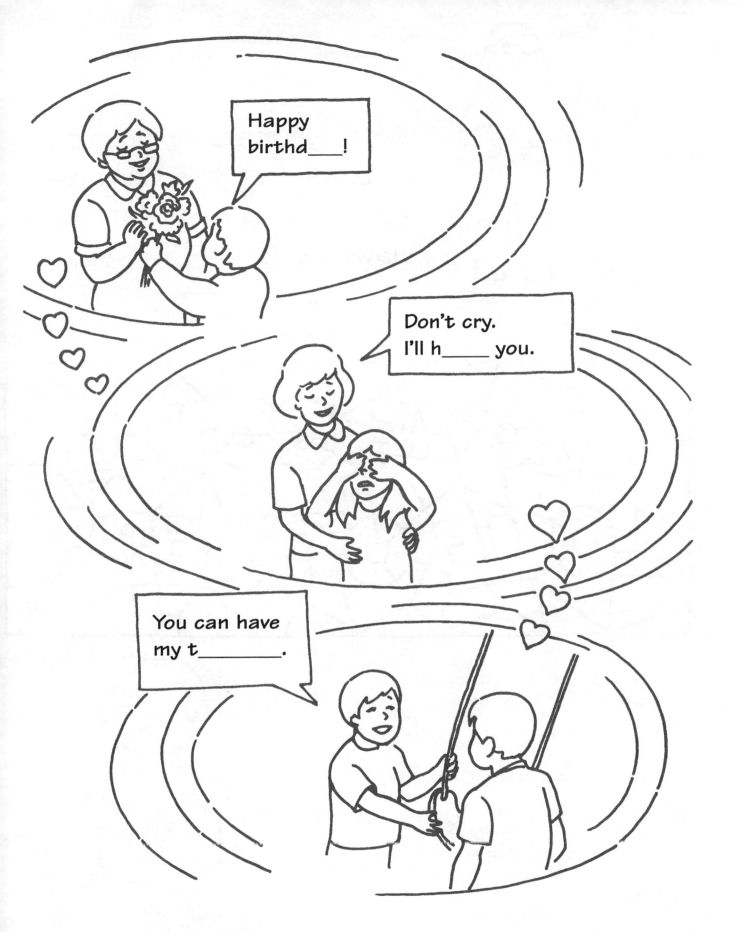

The good things we do are like r_____ of l_____.

When we make ripples of love, we keep the two great commandments that Jesus gave us.

When we make ripples of love, we let others know how much God loves them.

What ripples of love will you make this week?

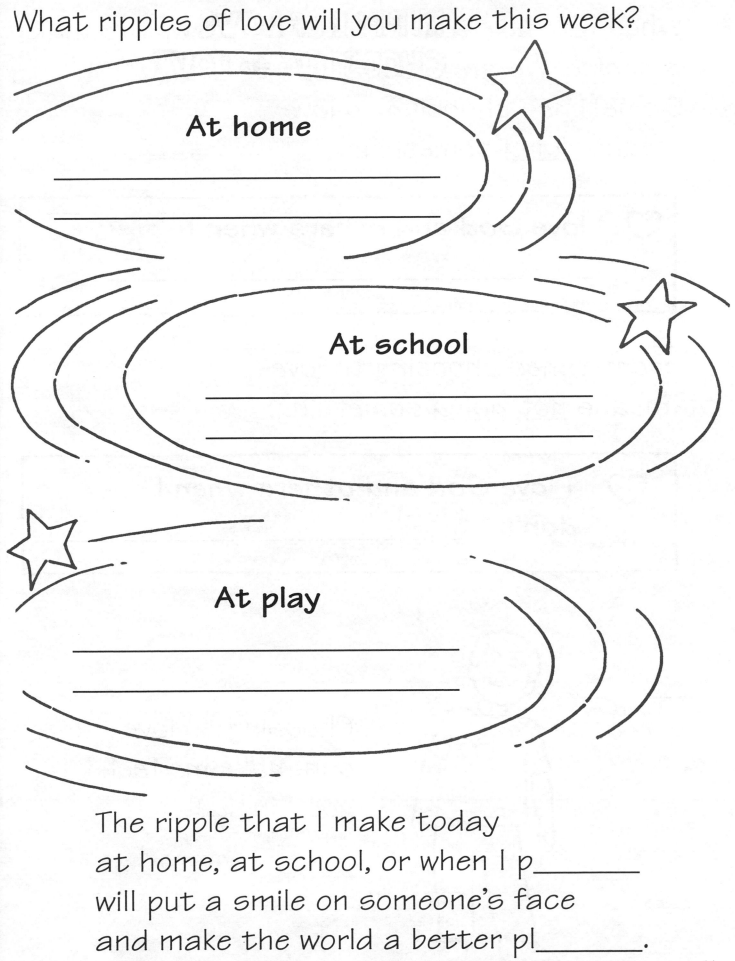

At home

_____

_____

At school

_____

_____

At play

_____

_____

The ripple that I make today
at home, at school, or when I p_____
will put a smile on someone's face
and make the world a better pl_____.

11

When we make a **RIPPLE of LOVE** we are making a choice. We are **CHOOSING to LOVE.**
Sometimes choosing to love means <u>doing</u> something.

♡ **I love God and others when I**

_____ .

Sometimes choosing to love means <u>not</u> <u>doing</u> something.

♡ **I love God and others when I don't** _____ .

Choosing to love can make me feel good inside!

God helps us make good choices.

☆ God gives us special people to teach us how to be loving.

___ mother   ___ teacher

___ father   ___ priest

___ _____

☆ God also gives us the Bible to guide us

What are some of the things the Bible tells us?

(Begin with the letter at the top of the circle and choose every other letter until all the spaces are filled.)

____ ____

____ ____

____ ____

____

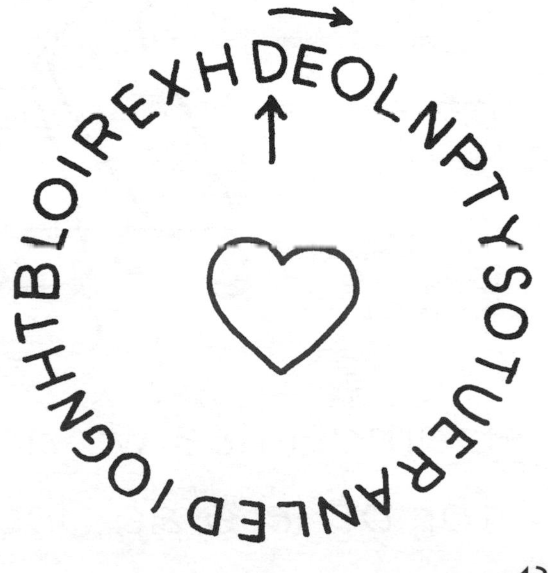

Most of the time we try to love God and others
the best we can.
    But sometimes we get selfish.
Sometimes what <u>we</u> want seems more important
than loving God and others.

Sometimes we do not show love and concern
for others as Jesus did.

Can you think of a time when you did something wrong <u>on</u> <u>purpose</u>?

How did you feel inside?

_____

How do you think the people around you felt?

_____

The bad things we do affect others.

_____

When we choose to do what <u>we</u> <u>want</u> instead of what <u>God</u> <u>wants</u>, we call it <u>sin</u>.

Sin is something wrong that we do o__ p_____.
Sin is against G____ and o_____.

We sin when we <u>refuse</u> to show love for God and others and we know we should.

Sin h_____ others
and it weakens my friendship
with G___.

Sin also pulls me away from a loving
closeness with my b_____
and s_____ in God's
family.

When we sin, we sometimes feel alone and scared.
We wish we could make things right again.
But how?

Making things right again begins by being

for what we did wrong.

Saying "I'm sorry"
can help make things
right again.

In the Bible, a tax collector named Zacchaeus showed he was sorry for cheating people out of their money by giving them back 4 times what he took!

Doing something to make up for what we did wrong can also help make things right again.

When we sin, we weaken our friendship with God. Does God stop loving us? How can we make things right again with God?

Jesus told a story to help answer these questions.

Once there was a shepherd who had 100 sheep. Every day he watched over his sheep and kept them safe.

Every night he counted his sheep to make sure they were all there. He was a good shepherd.

One day one of the sheep wandered away and got lost.

That night when the shepherd counted his sheep, he discovered that one was missing!

He was very worried and went to look for it right away.

When the shepherd found the lost sheep, he was <u>very</u> happy. He put it on his shoulders and went home with great joy.

Draw a picture of the celebration.

When he arrived home, he invited everyone to celebrate with him because he found his lost sheep.

At the end of the story Jesus said, "There will be more joy in heaven over **1** sinner who repents than over **99** who do not need to."

When we sin, we are like s __ __ __ __ that wander away from God's love.

Jesus is like the good s __ __ __ __ __ __ __ __. He wants to find us and bring us back home.

When we tell him that we are sorry for what we did, we let him know that we want to be found and forgiven.

God never stops loving us! God will al_____ forgive us when we are s_____ for what we did, no matter how bad it was.

23

ISN'T IT GREAT THAT GOD LOVES US SO MUCH!

The **ACT OF CONTRITION** is a prayer that tells God we are sorry and want to make things right again.

1. My God,
I am s_____ for my sins
with all my h_____.
2. In c_____ to do wrong
and failing to do g_____
I have sinned against you
whom I should l_____
above all things.
3. I firmly intend,
with your help,
to do p_____,
to sin no more,
and to a_____
whatever leads me to sin.
4. Our Savior J_____ Christ
suffered and died for us.
In his name, my God,
have mercy. Amen.

Jesus

love

choosing

penance

heart

avoid

good

sorry

"Contrition" means <u>to be sorry</u>.

God wants each person
in his family to be
like a 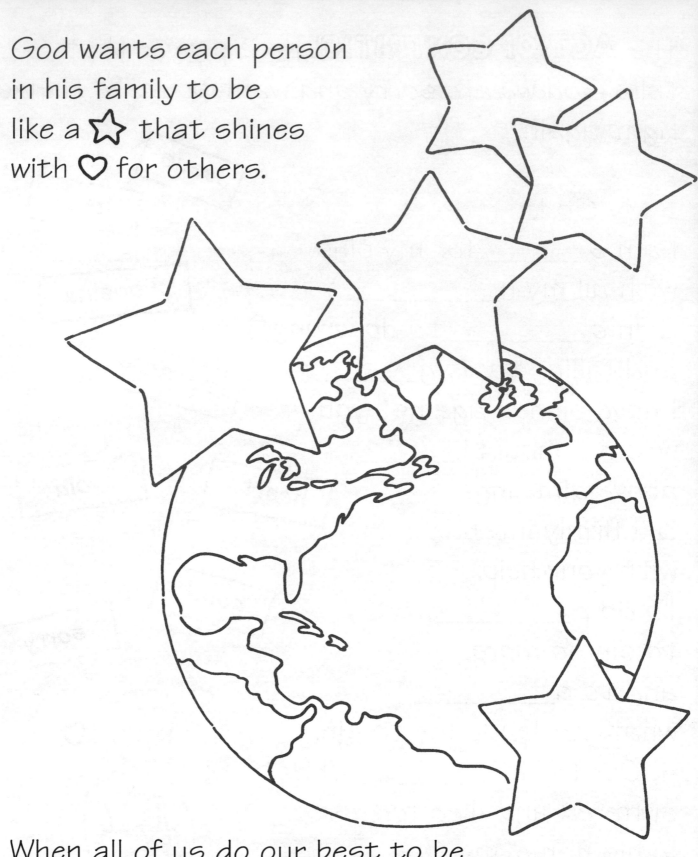 that shines
with ♡ for others.

When all of us do our best to be
kind and live at peace with one another, we
light up the world with Jesus' ♡.
What did you do today? _____

When we refuse to be loving, when we fight or disobey or lie, our ☆ doesn't shine as brightly as it should and . . .

. . . we pull away from a loving closeness with others in God's family.

When we sin, we need to ask God and our brothers and sisters to <u>forgive</u> us and help us keep the light of Jesus' ♡ in our hearts.

We need the

SACRAMENT
OF
RECONCILIATION

to bring us <u>together</u> again.

"Reconciliation" is a big word that means

being friends again.

Find your way from sadness to gladness with your pencil.

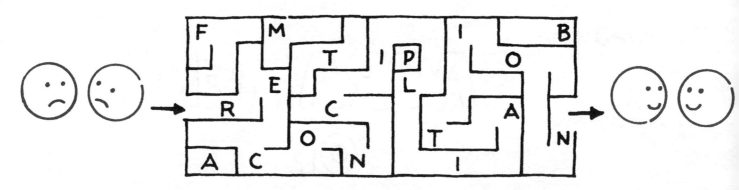

What letters did your line go through?

_ _ _ _ _ _ _ _ _ _ _ _ _ _

THE SACRAMENT OF RECONCILIATION

is one of the special ways
that God shows his love for us.

When we celebrate the
Sacrament of Reconciliation,
our sins are forgiven through
the power of Jesus' love.

Jesus' love brings us
all together again as
one family.

God
and ___
and
others

And that's a time to CELEBRATE!!

To get ready for the Sacrament of Reconciliation, we find a quiet place to think and pray.

We ask the Holy Spirit to help us look at our lives.

- At home
- At school
- After school
- At play

Was I like Jesus?
Did I love God and others?
Did I help others when they needed it?
Did I hurt anyone by what I said or did?
Did I think about God and remember to pray?

We tell God we are s_____ for our sins.
We ask him to help us learn to be b_____.

When we are ready to celebrate the Sacrament of Reconciliation, we gather together in the church.

The priest welcomes us with love and understanding.

He wants to help us receive God's forgiveness and reconciliation.

We begin our celebration by s____ing and p____ing together.

We listen to readings from the B_____.

"Rejoice with me because I have found my lost s_____."

God's words have the power to change our hearts.

The priest helps us think about what we did wrong.

We are all sorry we have sinned against God and others.

We pray for forgiveness.

Draw a picture offering a sign of peace.

We say the
O_____
F_____
together and offer each other a sign of
p_____.

Then we are invited to go to the priest to confess our sins.

"Confess" means to t_____.

When it is my turn to talk with the priest, this is what happens.

The priest is happy to see me. He is like the shepherd in the story of the lost s __ __ __ __.

We begin with the Sign of the Cross. I tell him that this is my first confession.

I tell him about the times I did not love God and others. He listens and understands. He is big now, but once he was a child like me.

Sometimes we talk about what I did wrong and try to figure out how I can change and be more like Jesus.

Then the priest asks me to do something to help make up for what I did and to help me grow in love. This is called a <u>penance</u>.

Then the priest forgives my sins through the love of Jesus and the power of the Holy Spirit.

I absolve you from your sins in the name of the Father, and of the Son, and of the Holy Spirit.

The priest's words of forgiveness bring me very close to God and my brothers and sisters.

JOY

When the celebration of the Sacrament of Reconciliation ends, our hearts are filled with joy.

Can you match these?

Jesus' love for us . . .	for his mercy.
We are all together again . . .	has taken away all our sins.
We praise and thank God . . .	in peace and friendship.

Sometimes I feel just like I've been

HUGGED BY GOD!

The Sacrament of Reconciliation is
a **NEW BEGINNING** for us.

God's love and forgiveness give us new strength
to live as his children.

With God's help
we can change
selfishness
to k_____ness

With God's help we can g_____ in love.

We grow in love when we do our best to

__ __ __ __ __ __ __ __ __ __ __ every day.

2 5 4 4 5 8   3 1 6 7 6

1 = e   2 = f   3 = J   4 = l   5 = o   6 = s   7 = u   8 = w

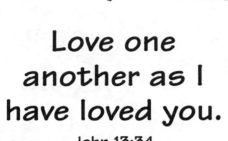

Love one
another as I
have loved you.

John 13:34

What can you do to grow in love today?

_____

_____

Growing in love isn't always easy.
Even though we try hard to do the right thing,
sometimes we may sin.

We may need to say "I'm sorry" and try to
make things right over and over again.

But no matter how many times we wander away from his love, God is <u>always</u> ready to forgive us and bring us back home.

_____, ___ _____ _____, **can stop God from loving us!**
(sins our even not Nothing)

God gave us the
SACRAMENT of RECONCILIATION
for our **WHOLE** life.

We never get too
o____ for God's
l____ and mercy!

Anytime we need God's forgiveness and grace to make things right again, the **SACRAMENT OF RECONCILIATION** is there for us.

It brings us the p_____ that comes with God's forgiveness . . .

. . . and the l____ we need to begin again.

THANK YOU, GOD!

MAKING THINGS RIGHT
PARENT/CATECHIST GUIDE

BACKGROUND

The Sacrament of Reconciliation is given to us through the love of Jesus and through the Church. It addresses one of our most common human experiences — the need for forgiveness and reconciliation. In the Sacrament of Reconciliation, God forgives our sins and draws us near to himself in love and reconciliation. He heals our wounds, gives us a sense of inner peace, and unites us again with the Christian community.

Although sin is the reason we have the Sacrament of Reconciliation, in reality the sacrament is more about God's unbelievable love and mercy than about sin. The parable of the Prodigal Son tells us that God welcomes the contrite with open arms, just as the father in the parable welcomed his repentant son. God's love is never withdrawn — no matter what we have done! We are still his sons and daughters, and his forgiveness is always waiting for us.

Sin is a part of everyone's life. As the First Letter of John says, "If we say we have no sin, we deceive ourselves" (1 John 1:8). Sin has many familiar faces — gossip, lying, deception, laziness, unfaithfulness, discrimination, neglecting our responsibilities to God, and much more. Sin also includes the things we do not do — things that Christians are called to do, such as speaking up in the face of injustice or helping those in need. Some describe sin as a kind of selfishness, a turning inward on ourselves rather than turning outward toward God and others.

> The LORD is gracious and merciful, slow to anger and abounding in steadfast love.
> — Psalm 145:8

Sin is destructive to our relationship with God, who is deserving of all our love. The *Catechism of the Catholic Church* tells us that sin "sets itself against God's love for us and turns our hearts away from it" (n. 1850). Mortal sins — sins that involve serious acts, sins that are done with full knowledge and will — shut the doors of our hearts to God. But even when we cut ourselves off from God's grace through mortal sin, God continues to love us and longs to bring us back. Lesser, or venial, sins weaken our relationship with God and sometimes pave the path to more serious sins.

Not only is our relationship with God affected by sin, but our other relationships are affected also. Relationships with family, friends, or co-workers grow cold and sometimes are broken. Our casual relationships with, for example, clerks and repair persons are tainted, and our relationship with the environment is affected by waste or abuse of natural resources. Sin also affects our relationship with ourselves. It makes us less whole — and less holy. Finally, sin has an affect on the entire Christian community. As baptized persons, we are called to make Christ present in our world. Sinful actions work against this, and they lead people away from, rather than toward, Christ. When we sin, we need forgiveness, *and* we need to be reconciled with our brothers and sisters in God's family.

Approaching the Sacrament of Reconciliation calls for honesty and humility in admitting that we have failed to live as we should. It also calls for heartfelt sorrow for our sins and a sincere desire to change. These are the essentials for opening the door to God's mercy and grace in the sacrament.

The priest is the minister of the sacrament. He has been given the power to forgive sins and to reconcile sinners to God and the community through the Sacrament of Holy Orders. He acts in the person of Christ and as a representative of the community that has been wounded by our sins. When we confess our sins, he accepts us as we are, listens with the compassion and understanding of Christ, guides us and supports our desire to change by assigning a penance, and heals us through the words of absolution:

God, the Father of mercies,
through the death and resurrection of his Son
has reconciled the world to himself
and sent the Holy Spirit among us
for the forgiveness of sins;
through the ministry of the Church
may God give you pardon and peace,
and I absolve you from your sins
in the name of the Father, and of the Son,
and of the Holy Spirit.
— Rite of Penance (n. 46)

Along with offering opportunities to celebrate the Sacrament of Reconciliation as individuals, most parishes today also offer communal celebrations of Reconciliation with individual confession and absolution, especially during Advent and Lent. These celebrations make the communal nature of sin and reconciliation obvious. When we come together in prayer, we are united in knowing that we have sinned, in our need for forgiveness and reconciliation, and in our desire to change.

COMMUNAL CELEBRATION

Introductory Rites
- Song
- Greeting
- Opening Prayer

Celebration of the Word of God
- Readings from Scripture
- Homily
- Examination of Conscience

Rite of Reconciliation
- General Confession of Sins and the Lord's Prayer
- Individual Confession and Absolution
- Proclamation of Praise
- Prayer of Thanksgiving

Concluding Rite

Readings from Scripture and the words of the homily are an important part of communal celebrations of Reconciliation. They call us to conversion and help us examine our lives in light of our responsibilities as Catholic Christians and in light of God's mercy. After the "celebration of the Word of God," penitents are invited to confess their sins to a priest — either face-to-face or behind a screen — and to receive sacramental absolution. Persons who participate in communal celebrations but do not confess their sins to a priest may receive many benefits, including God's forgiveness. However, confession to a priest is essential for celebrating the Sacrament of Reconciliation.

The Sacrament of Reconciliation is a special gift — an important help in the lifelong process of conversion. It calls us to thoughtful reflection on our lives and offers the prayerful support of the community as we renew our efforts to live our baptismal call. It highlights God's love and mercy, and it gives us the grace to put Christ at the center of our lives again. It also helps satisfy our human need for personal assurance that we are loved and forgiven by God. We hear with our own ears the words of forgiveness that release us from the burden of sin, restore us to wholeness, give us a sense of inner peace, and strengthen us to begin again.

INTRODUCTION TO "MAKING THINGS RIGHT"

Making Things Right is designed to help children in grades two, three, or four prepare for their first experience of God's love and mercy in the Sacrament of Reconciliation — either in the home or in a classroom situation. It can also be used with children who have already made their first confession to help them come to a deeper understanding and appreciation of the sacrament and its place in their lives.

Making Things Right approaches the preparation and celebration of the Sacrament of Reconciliation in a positive way, weaving God's constant and forgiving love throughout. It meets children in their world, builds on their experiences, and helps them come to a better understanding of themselves, their relationship with a loving God, and their relationship with the people around them. It encourages them to grow in love for God and others by following the example of Jesus. Sin and its effects are discussed with sensitivity, and the children are led step-by-step through the reconciliation process. The communal celebration of the Sacrament of Reconciliation is presented as part of the whole process of "making things right."

There are seven natural divisions of the material in *Making Things Right*. In a classroom setting, allowing time for review, enrichment, etc., the preparation will extend over a minimum of seven sessions — six before and one after the celebration of the sacrament. Before beginning each new section, the preceding material should be reviewed briefly in order to reinforce learning and provide continuity.

Making Things Right includes many activities that catch the interest of children. Consequently, they may want to rush to complete them before they have an understanding of what they are about. One way to direct but not dampen their enthusiasm is to talk about the section to be covered — either with or without the book — in a place separate from the usual work area. When the discussion is finished, the children can move to the work area to complete the corresponding material in the book.

As children use *Making Things Right*, they should be encouraged to make it their own by underlining or circling words that are meaningful to them, coloring the illustrations, filling in the open letters, and adding personal touches. Allowing children time to color the illustrations is important since it helps them reflect on the material.

The guide that follows provides page-by-page assistance for both parents and catechists. It gives background for the ideas presented, suggests possible approaches to use with children, offers practical suggestions, and recommends ways that topics can be enriched to meet individual needs, enhance learning, or make the sessions more enjoyable.

PARENT/CATECHIST GUIDE

PAGE 1: This introductory page helps stimulate the interest of children in learning how to make things right again by suggesting a situation that most children can relate to — being alone and sad, and wondering what to do after having done something wrong.

> • Look at the illustration with the children and invite them to imagine why the girl is sitting by herself. Ask them how they think she feels and if they have ever felt like that. You may want to tell them about a similar experience you had when you were a child and share how you felt.
> • Conclude by reading the sentence with the children.

SECTION 1: PAGES 2-7 FOCUS ON HELPING CHILDREN RECOGNIZE OUR SPECIAL RELATIONSHIP WITH GOD AND ONE ANOTHER AND LEARN HOW TO LIVE AS GOD WANTS US TO LIVE.

PAGE 2: Our perception of our own worth is a major factor in determining the quality of our relationships with others — including our relationship with God. This page encourages children to feel good about themselves, awakens in them a sense of their uniqueness, and leads them to an awareness of the great love that God has for each and every one of us.

Preparation: Read Matthew 10:29-31.

> • Ask the children to write their name and age in the space provided. Invite them to either draw or attach a picture of themselves in the frame and to check the activities that they like to do. They may want to add something else on the blank line.
> • Invite them to share what they like to do best and help them appreciate the fact that each of us is "one-of-a-kind" and each of us is loved by God.
> • Read the sentence at the bottom of the page. Reinforce how precious we are in God's sight by telling the children what Jesus said about the importance of two sparrows (Matthew 10:29-31).

Missing words: Child's name, age, activities that he or she likes to do.

Activities: Children draw or attach pictures of themselves in the frame. Color "GOD LOVES ME!"

PAGE 3: God calls us into a special grace-filled relationship at Baptism. He is our Father and we are his children. As members of his family, the Church, we are all brothers and sisters of one another. This page draws the children's attention to their Baptism and explores its meaning. In discussing this and other pages with children, it is important to be sensitive to the variety of families in which they live.

Preparation: Arrange Baptism symbols, a bowl of water and a candle, on a table with a cloth.

• Talk with the children about their experiences of belonging to a family. Invite them to share how their parents, stepparents or guardians, brothers and sisters, and other close relatives show their love for them. Ask the children what they do to show their love for the members of their family. Help them see that family living means giving as well as receiving love.

• Invite the children to share what they know about their Baptism. Ask them to have one of their parents put the date of their Baptism in their book when they go home.

• Tell them that God's love for them is so great that he made them part of his own family when they were baptized. Explain that "the Church" is the name we give to God's family, and that everyone who belongs to the Church is a child of God and has been filled with a new life of grace.

• Talk about how being part of God's family is like being part of our own family. Compare God's love and care for them with their parents' love and care for them.

• Help the children understand that all of the people in God's family are really our brothers and sisters, and that they also love us. Give examples of their love and care: praying for us and with us at Mass, helping us learn about Jesus, celebrating with us when special events like Baptisms and First Communions happen, and helping people when they need it.

• Read the page with the children and invite them to discover the message in the heart by darkening the "x" squares with their pencils.

Missing words: Date of child's baptism.
Message: God is our Father. We are all brothers and sisters.

PAGE 4: God's desire is for everyone in his family to love him and one another. This page helps children become aware of the many ways we can show love for God and one another, and it leads them to see that love is the path to true happiness.

Preparation: Cut out magazine pictures of people showing love for one another, or provide drawing materials for each child.

• Read the two sentences at the top of the page with the children. Invite them to give examples of ways we show love for God and ways we show love for one another. Help them think of examples by calling their attention to different areas of their life — home, school, and play. Add to them as needed. Emphasize the importance of being kind and learning to live at peace with one another.

• Give the children magazine pictures of people showing love for one another and have them put the pictures in the frame. (Or ask them to draw pictures of people being kind and loving to one another.)

• When they are finished, invite the children to talk about their pictures. Explain that loving God and others leads us to true and lasting happiness. Ask them to remember a time they did something for someone else that made them feel good inside.

• Read the Scripture passage at the bottom of the page and encourage the children to remember it.

Activity: Put a magazine picture or a drawing of people showing love for one another in the frame.

PAGE 5: Jesus showed us by his life what it means to love God and others. This page and the two that follow flow together to lead children to follow Jesus' example of love. Page 5 helps them become more aware of how Jesus loved and cared for others.

Preparation: Be familiar with the Scripture stories suggested by the picture and the activity:

- Curing the blind (Mark 10:46-52)
- Curing the sick (Luke 5:12-14 or John 5:1-9)
- Feeding people (John 6:1-14)
- Teaching to pray (Matthew 6:9-13)

Find a children's book with one of these stories: for example, *Stories and Songs of Jesus* by Paule Freeburg and Christopher Walker (OCP Publications).

- Read the sentence at the top of the page with the children and look at the picture. Invite someone to tell the story of Jesus curing the blind man, or tell it yourself. Talk with the children about how they would feel if they were blind and Jesus made them see again.

- Invite them to complete the sentences at the bottom of the page by drawing a line between the correct phrases. Read the completed sentences with them.

- Gather the children around you and read one of the Bible stories suggested in the activity. Talk about it and help the children come to an appreciation of how much Jesus loved others.

- If time permits, invite the children to color the picture of Jesus curing the blind man (or ask them to do it at home).

Completed sentences: He made blind people see again. He cured sick people. He fed the hungry crowd. He taught people how to pray.

Activity: Color the picture.

PAGES 6 AND 7: The challenge for all of us is to reflect Jesus' words and example in our own actions and attitudes. These two pages help children focus on what it means to "be like Jesus" in their daily lives.

Preparation: Make a small paper heart for each child — and a few extra.

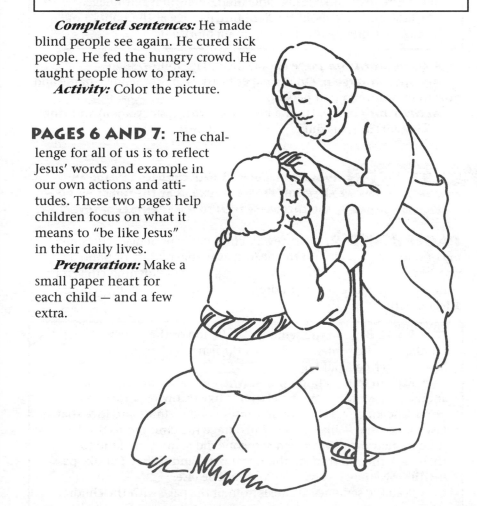

• **PAGE 6:** Read the sentences at the top of the page with the children.

• Invite them to find the five words in the "word search." When they have found them, invite them to use the words to complete the sentences below.

• Read and talk about each of the sentences. Try to relate them to the children's lives in personal and specific ways. For example, ask them how and when they pray, who needs help at their house, what they can do to help, when they should play fair, why following the rules at school is important, etc. Remind them that when they do these things, they are following Jesus' example.

• Look at the picture and read the sentence at the bottom of the page. Help the children understand that loving others is how we show that we love God. Encourage the children to memorize it.

• Distribute the paper hearts and invite the children to write the name of someone they know on it and something they will do to show their love for that person the next time they are with him or her. Encourage the children to put the heart in a special place at home as a reminder to "be like Jesus."

• **PAGE 7:** Read the sentences at the top of the page with the children and invite them to follow the instructions. Work individually with children who need help remembering when they were like Jesus.

• When the children are done, invite them to share their pictures or stories. Be generous with your praise. It will help reinforce their desire to "be like Jesus" and strengthen their self-image.

• Read and talk about the Scripture passage at the bottom of the page. Encourage the children to memorize it.

Missing words on page 6: pray, help, fair, follow, share.

Activity on page 6: On the paper heart, write someone's name and how to show love to that person.

Activity on page 7: Draw a picture or write a story about showing love for others as Jesus did.

SECTION 2: PAGES 8 THROUGH 13 HELP CHILDREN DEVELOP AN AWARENESS OF HOW WE AFFECT THE PEOPLE AROUND US BY THE THINGS WE DO — BOTH GOOD AND BAD — AND ENCOURAGE THEM TO MAKE "RIPPLES OF LOVE."

PAGES 8 AND 9: Nearly every child has experienced the simple joy of throwing a rock into the nearest available puddle or pond and watching the ripples as they race outward in ever-widening circles. This common experience helps children understand how loving actions affect others.

• **PAGE 8:** Read the sentence at the top of the page with the children. Invite someone who has thrown a rock into a pond or lake to describe what happens.

• Explain to the children that when we do something that shows our love for someone else, it is like throwing a rock into a pond. The kindness that we do causes good feelings and love that last a long time — like ripples. Encourage the children to think of a time in their own lives when someone did something kind to them. Ask them if it made them feel good and if they felt like passing the love they received on to someone else.

• Read the sentence at the bottom of the page with the children.

• **PAGE 9:** Look at the three pictures on the page with the children. Invite them to describe what they see happening and help them fill in the blanks. Point out that the people in the pictures are making "ripples of love."

• Help the children become aware of other ways to make "ripples of love" by inviting them to dramatize situations such as these:

— "Imagine that you are watching TV and your little brother begins to cry because he can't find his favorite blanket."

— "Imagine it is lunchtime and your friend tells you that he lost his lunch money."

— "Imagine that there is a new child in your class."

(This kind of activity is fun for the children and helps them grow in their ability to recognize and respond to the needs of others.)

• Read the sentence at the bottom of the page and help the children fill in the blanks.

Missing words on page 9: birthday, help, turn, ripples, love.

PAGES 10 AND 11: These two pages help children understand and relate the two great commandments to each other and to "ripples of love," and they encourage the children to make their own "ripples of love."

• **PAGE 10:** Talk with the children about the two great commandments that Jesus gave us. Ask them to give examples of how we love God and how we love others.

• Help them understand that the two great commandments are connected. Whenever we love others, we are showing our love for God — and when we love God, we will love others, too.

• Call the children's attention to the puzzle in the center of the page and invite them to find the two great commandments by coloring or shading in the dotted areas.

• Read the sentence at the top of the page with the children. Use examples to show how making "ripples of love" is the same as keeping the two great commandments.

• Read the sentence at the bottom of the page with the children. Help them understand that God uses our love for others to show them that he loves them. Our love becomes a sign of God's love for them.

• **PAGE 11:** Look at the page with the children. Invite them to try very hard during the next week to make "ripples of love." Show them how they can keep a record of the "ripples of love" that they make at home, at school, and when they play. Encourage them to make as many ripples as they can!

• Read the poem at the bottom of the page together and help the children complete the missing words. (When you come together the next time, invite the children to share the "ripples of love" that they made and read the poem at the bottom of the page again.)

Hidden words on page 10: LOVE GOD, LOVE OTHERS.
Activity on page 11: Keep a record of "ripples of love."
Missing words on page 11: play, place.

PAGES 12 AND 13: Learning to make good choices is an important part of moral formation. These pages help children associate making "ripples of love" with making good choices and lead them to understand how God helps them learn to make good choices.

Preparation: Bring a Bible.

• **PAGE 12:** Invite the children to gather around you and talk with them about the choices that they make every day: what to wear to school, what to eat for breakfast, what friend to play with at recess, what book to read, etc.

• Remind the children that Jesus always made good choices, and that God wants us to make good choices, too. Use the "ripples of love" on page 9 to show them that making a "ripple of love" is really the same as choosing to love.

• Explain to them that sometimes choosing to love means *doing* something and sometimes it means *not doing* something. Ask the children for examples of choices that involve doing something — for example, offering to help someone when they fall down, loaning someone a pencil, or offering to help their mother or father when they are tired. Then ask them for examples of choosing to love that mean *not doing* something — for example, not lying, not cheating, not putting someone down, or not calling a person a bad name.

• Read the page with the children and help them complete the sentences.

• Read the last sentence on the page and talk with the children about the good feelings that can come from making good choices. If time permits, read *The Little Brute Family* by Russell Hoban (Macmillan). This story tells about a good feeling that made a big difference in the Brute family's life.

• **PAGE 13:** Talk with the children about how they learn to make good choices. Explain that God helps them through other people. Invite them to share how their parents and others guide and teach them to make good choices.

• Read the page with the children. Ask them to check the people who teach them how to make good choices. Invite them to add the name of someone else in the space provided.

• Show the children the Bible and tell them that God also gave us the Bible to help us learn how to make good choices. Explain that the stories Jesus told, the things he did, his teachings, and the teachings of his apostles — all of which we find in the Bible — help guide us.

• Help the children discover what the Bible tells us at the bottom of the page. If time permits, read or tell the story of the Good Samaritan (Luke 10:29-37) to illustrate the meaning of "neighbor."

Activity on page 12: Complete the sentences.

Missing words on page 13: Name of another person who teaches and guides them.

Puzzle on page 13: Don't steal. Don't lie. Help your neighbor.

SECTION 3: PAGES 14-19 FOCUS ON THE TIMES WE DO NOT LOVE AS WE SHOULD. CHILDREN ARE LED TO UNDERSTAND THE MEANING OF SIN AND ITS EFFECT ON OUR RELATIONSHIPS, AND THEY ARE INTRODUCED TO THE STEPS FOR "MAKING THINGS RIGHT" AGAIN.

PAGES 14 AND 15: Try as we may, at times all of us fail to be as caring and compassionate as we should be. As children reflect on this reality, they are led to discover that just as the good things we do affect others, the bad choices we make also affect them.

The following optional activity may be used to introduce the material on page 14.

Preparation: Prepare slips of paper with various situations written on them that represent things the children might be tempted to do. Some examples are:

- "Finish the game even though your mother called to you."
- "Go play instead of helping clean up the table after dinner."
- "Hide your candy instead of sharing it."
- "Say you don't feel well when you have homework to do."
- "Tell your sister it was your turn to choose first when it really wasn't."
- "Keep the ring you found on the playground."

Make enough slips of paper for each child and put them in a basket.

• PAGE 14: Gather the children around the basket and invite them to take turns selecting and reading the slips of paper. As the situations are read, ask the group if they have ever been tempted to do something like that. Then ask what they think God would want them to do. Help them see that when we do what we want instead of what God wants, we are thinking only of ourselves.

• Read the sentences at the top of the page with the children and talk about the picture. Ask them to write what they think the children are saying to each other. When they are finished, invite them to share what they wrote.

• Read the sentence at the bottom of the page and ask the children what they think Jesus would do in this situation.

• PAGE 15: Read the sentence at the top of the page with the children. Ask them to close their eyes and think about (or imagine) a time when they did something that was wrong *on purpose*. (Emphasize that it should be something that was wrong that was done deliberately, not accidentally).

• Ask them to think about how they felt inside. Give them a little time and then ask them to think about how the people around them felt — perhaps their parents, stepparents or guardian, a teacher, a friend, or a brother or sister.

• Ask them to open their eyes and invite them to draw a mouth on the large face (which represents them) to show how they felt and, beneath the face, to write a word or two that expresses how they felt. Then invite them to do the same thing for the smaller faces (which represent the people affected by what they did).

• Invite the children to share how they felt and how the people around them felt. (Focus on the feelings rather than what was done. Be careful not impose the "right" feelings on the children.)

• Help them understand that sometimes when we do what we want and not what God wants, we end up feeling empty, sad, lonely, or afraid — and the people around us also feel bad.

• Draw their attention to the picture at the bottom of the page and ask if they remember seeing it before. Help them understand that just as our "ripples of love" affect other people, the bad things we do also affect others.

• If time permits, read *The Quarreling Book* by Charlotte Zolotow (Harper and Row) to illustrate how we affect one another by what we do.

Activity on page 14: Write what the children are saying to one another.

Activity on page 15: Draw expressions on the faces. Describe the feelings below the faces.

PAGE 16: Helping children come to an initial understanding of sin needs to be done with care. In working with children, it is important to help them realize that sin is not the same as simply doing something wrong. Sin is doing something wrong *on purpose*. Children should be led to distinguish sin from accidents and mistakes, and to understand that sin comes from inside us — from our refusal to love God and others. Sin is against love for God and others. It is the result of choosing to put what we want first. The sentence on the bottom of the page is a beginning description of sin for children.

Preparation: On small pieces of paper, write examples of sins, accidents, and mistakes common to children. Include at least one accident that either injures someone or breaks something. Put them in a basket.

> • Read the sentence at the top of the page with the children. Look at the picture with them and talk about what they think is happening. Suggested questions to ask are:
> — What is the girl saying to the other child? (Write her words in the "bubble.")
> — Are the two children leaving the girl out of their play on purpose?
> — Have they ever seen children do that before?
> — Are the two children doing what God wants or what they want?
> Explain that this is an example of what we call "sin." Emphasize that sin is something wrong that we do *on purpose*.
> • Help the children clarify the difference between sins, accidents, and mistakes by inviting them to choose papers from the basket you prepared and say whether the action is a sin, an accident, or a mistake. Help the children understand that when we commit a sin we are deliberately choosing to do what we want to do instead of what God wants.
> • Invite the children to fill in the missing words in the sentences at the bottom of the page.
> • Read the sentence in the box and help the children understand that the word "refuse" means *not doing something on purpose.* Finally, explain that for something to be a sin we also need to know that what we are doing is wrong. For example, when babies do things that are wrong, like throwing food on the floor, they don't sin because they don't know that it is wrong yet.

Missing words: on, purpose, God, others.

PAGE 17: This page addresses the effects of sin. The most obvious effect is that others are hurt — sometimes physically and other times emotionally. Sin also affects our relationship with God since our love for God is intimately bound up with our love for others. Finally, sin affects our relationship with the people in God's family. Just as the good we do draws us closer to them, our sinfulness pulls us away from them.

• Look at the picture on the page with the children and talk with them about it. Ask them if they think the two children who deliberately left the girl out of their play saw her crying.

• Explain that sin hurts others. Sometimes it hurts them physically — for example, when children fight with one another — and sometimes it hurts them on the inside. Ask them to give examples of sins that hurt other people's feelings. (Name-calling and teasing are common among children.)

• Help the children understand that sin also hurts our friendship with God because our love for God and our love for others are connected. When we sin, we are telling God by our actions that what he wants isn't very important to us.

• Finally, explain that sin separates us from the rest of God's family. Call the children's attention to the girl sitting by herself at the bottom of the page. Explain that when we let the things we want push love for God and others out of our heart, the only person we are close to is ourself.

• Help the children fill in the missing words and read the completed sentences.

• If time permits, read *The Hurt* by Teddi Doleski (Paulist Press). It tells the story of a little boy who was hurt by the name his friend called him.

Missing words: hurts, God, brothers, sisters.

PAGE 18: The process of reconciliation is a process of healing our relationships — with God and with each other. The first step is being sorry for what we did. Both children and adults often find it difficult to face the person they hurt, admit their guilt, and ask for forgiveness.

• Look at the picture and read the sentences at the top of the page with the children. Talk with them about their experiences of feeling lonely, confused, or scared because of something they did. Ask them to suggest ways to make things right again.

• Invite the children to tell about a time they told someone they were sorry — or share one of your experiences. Ask them if anyone has ever told them they were sorry. What did they do? Tell them that saying you are sorry to someone is the same as asking them to forgive you.

• Talk about whether it is easy or difficult to say you're sorry to the person you hurt. Tell the children that even adults sometimes find it difficult. Invite them to think of other ways to say they're sorry (for example, writing a note, doing something nice for the person, or giving someone a hug).

• Ask the children to say "I'm sorry" together. Then invite them to say it individually and listen to how they sound when they say "I'm sorry." Help the children understand that these are powerful words. They let the other person know that we want to be friends again.

• Invite the children to complete the activities on the page and then read it with them.

Activities: Connect the dots to form the word "SORRY." Write the words that one girl is using to ask the other girl to forgive her.

PAGE 19: Making up for the harm that we have done through sin is the second step in the process of "making things right." It is integral not only to reconciliation between individuals but also to the Sacrament of Reconciliation. The sacrament is not an easy way out, a way to avoid facing up to what we have done and what we need to do to make it right. Our efforts to be reconciled with God must begin with the person we hurt.

Preparation: Be able to tell the story of Zacchaeus (Luke 19:1-10), or find a children's book that tells it. (The story of Zacchaeus is simple enough to read directly from the Bible.)

• Help the children understand that when we sin we need to try to make up for any harm or damage that we did. Explain that making up for something we have done by doing something for the person or persons we hurt is a sign of our love and our sincerity.

• Give the children some examples of sinful acts — such as taking something from someone, cheating in a game, or deliberately ruining something that belongs to someone else — and ask them to suggest ways to make up for them. Explain that it is very difficult to make up for some sins — for example, telling a lie about someone.

• Tell or read the story of Zacchaeus. Talk about how Jesus' love for Zacchaeus helped him do the right thing. Assure the children that Jesus' love for us helps us do the right thing, too.

• Read the page with the children. Invite them to write what Zacchaeus is saying and to complete and color the picture.

Activities: Write what Zacchaeus is saying, connect the dots, and color the picture.

SECTION 4: PAGES 20-25 FOCUS ON REPAIRING OUR RELATIONSHIP WITH GOD. THEY EMPHASIZE GOD'S NEVER-ENDING LOVE FOR US THROUGH THE STORY OF THE LOST SHEEP.

PAGES 20-23: Because of our personal experiences, it is natural for us to wonder whether God still loves us when we sin, whether he will really forgive our sins, and whether we can ever be close again. Through the retelling of the parable of the Lost Sheep (Luke 15:4-7), the children are led to understand that God never stops loving us no matter what we do. God always longs to bring us back home.

• **PAGE 20:** Read the sentence and the questions at the top of the page with the children. Ask them if they have ever wondered about questions like these.

• **PAGES 20-22:** Read the parable of the Lost Sheep on pages 20-22 with them. Invite the children to fill in the "bubbles" as you read. At the end of the story, invite them to draw a picture of the good shepherd having a party with his friends after he found his lost sheep.

Talk about the parable using questions such as these:
— Do you think the sheep wandered off on purpose?
— How did the sheep feel when it began to get dark?
— Why do you think the shepherd left all of his other sheep to find the lost one?
— What do you think the shepherd did when he saw his lost sheep?
— Why do you think Jesus told us this story?

• Help the children understand that when we sin we are like the sheep that wandered off. Explain that Jesus loves us so much that he comes to look for us and brings us back to God who forgives our sins.

• Ask the children what they think "being forgiven" means. Invite them to share their experiences of being forgiven by parents and others. Ask them how they felt when they were forgiven. Point out that being forgiven can change us from feeling sad to feeling joyful.

• **PAGE 23:** Read the page with the children and help them complete the sentences. Emphasize that there is no sin so bad that God will not forgive it when we are sorry. God wants us to be close to him no matter what we have done, and he is always ready to give us another chance.

• If time permits, read *You Wouldn't Love Me If You Knew* by Jeannie St. John Taylor (Abingdon Press). It tells the story of a little boy who worries about being loved after he does something wrong.

Activities on pages 20 and 21: Write what the good shepherd is saying.

Activity on page 22: Draw a picture of the celebration.

Activity on page 23: Write what the lost sheep is saying — for example, "I'm lost," "I'm scared," or "Baaa!"

Missing words on page 23: sheep, shepherd, always, sorry.

PAGE 24: This page expresses the joy we feel when we begin to realize the depth of God's love for us, especially as shown by his willingness to forgive our sins.

• Read the page with the children and invite them to decorate the page in a joyful way. You may want to play some joyful music in the background as they work.

• When everyone is finished, invite the children to pray the litany below in thanksgiving for God's love and mercy. Ask the children to respond to each line with "Give thanks to the Lord for he is good" and end the litany with "Amen."

> God our Father, we thank you for making us part of your family, the Church.
> We thank you for giving us Jesus to teach us how to love you and others.
> We thank you for helping us make "ripples of love."
> We thank you for always loving us and forgiving us — even when we do wrong.
> Amen.

Activity: Decorate the page.

PAGE 25: Sorrow for sin may be expressed in our own words or by praying an Act of Contrition. This page introduces children to a widely used Act of Contrition.

> • Explain to the children that when we are sorry for our sins, we can ask God for forgiveness by praying a special prayer called an "Act of Contrition." Tell them that the word "contrition" means *to be sorry*.
> • Read the sentence at the top of the page with them. Then read the words down the right side of the page. Explain that the word "penance" refers to something we do to help make up for our sins and to help us grow in love. (Penance will be addressed again on page 36.)
> • Read each of the sentences and help the children find the correct words to fill in the blanks.
> • Pray the Act of Contrition together. Encourage the children to learn it and pray it at home.

Activity: Fill in the blanks with the correct words.

SECTION 5: PAGES 26-30 HELP CHILDREN UNDERSTAND OUR NEED TO BE RECONCILED WITH OUR BROTHERS AND SISTERS IN GOD'S FAMILY WHEN WE SIN. THESE PAGES INTRODUCE CHILDREN TO THE SACRAMENT OF RECONCILIATION AND HOW TO PREPARE FOR IT.

PAGES 26 AND 27: Our responsibility as members of the Church is to help make Jesus present in the world through our love and concern for others. Our sins obviously work against this. When we sin, we are less than we can be, Christ is less present in the world, and we distance ourselves from our brothers and sisters in Christ. Not only do we need God's forgiveness, we also need to be reconciled with the Church. These pages help children understand how sin affects our relationship with God's family and lead them to the Sacrament of Reconciliation.

Preparation: Find a children's book or a newspaper article about someone who made, or is making, a difference in the world by loving others, or invite someone from the parish to tell how he or she helps others through volunteer work.

Prepare to sing "This Little Light of Mine" with the children.

> • **PAGE 26:** Read the sentence at the top of the page with the children.
> • Invite them to put their name on one of the stars and the names of other children or family members on the other stars.
> • Explain that when we keep the two great commandments, we light up our part of the world with love. Invite the children to imagine what the world would be like if everyone kept these commandments. Explain that to fill the world with light and love, all people need to do their part.
> • Tell them a story, read a book, or invite someone from the parish to talk with them about what he or she does to bring Jesus' love to the world.
> • Read the sentences at the bottom of the page and ask the children to write what they did to help light up the world with Jesus' love. Invite them to share their good deeds and help them learn the song "This Little Light of Mine."

• **PAGE 27:** Explain to the children that our stars are powered by love. They shine brightly when we love God and others, and they grow dim when we sin. Explain that when we sin, we are not doing our part to light up the world with Jesus' love. Sin pulls us away from our brothers and sisters in God's family, and we need to ask for their forgiveness.

• Read the page with the children and invite them to connect the dots to form the star at the top of the page.

• Help them learn to pronounce "Sacrament of Reconciliation" and explain that it is through the Sacrament of Reconciliation that we receive God's forgiveness and make things right with our brothers and sisters in God's family.

• Invite the children to reflect on these pages by coloring them.

Activities on page 26: Write names on the stars. Answer the question at the bottom of the page. Color the page. Sing "This Little Light of Mine."

Activity on page 27: Connect the dots to form the star. Color the page.

PAGE 28: Reconciliation is the process of restoring the relationships damaged by sin — our relationship with God, with others, and with the Christian community. This page helps children understand and become comfortable with the word "reconciliation."

• Ask the children if they have ever had an argument with a friend and then made up with that friend later. Invite them to share what happened. Explain that making up with someone and being friends again is what the word "reconciliation" means.

• Read the page with the children and work with them to complete the maze activity.

• After they have written the word, ask the children to divide it into syllables to help them read and pronounce it (REC/ON/CIL/I/A/TION).

Activity: Find the way through the maze and write out (in order) the letters that the line went through.

PAGE 29: Sacraments are visible signs of God's love for us and sources of grace. In the Sacrament of Reconciliation, our sins are forgiven and we are reconciled with God and the Church through the mystery of Jesus' death and resurrection.

> • Talk with the children about the many ways that God shows his love for us.
>
> • Explain that God shows his love for us in special ways in the sacraments. Remind them that Baptism is a sacrament and ask them how God showed his love for us when we were baptized. (God made us part of his family and filled us with new life.) Tell them that in the Sacrament of Reconciliation God shows his love for us in another way — by forgiving our sins and bringing us close to him again in love.
>
> • Talk with them about Jesus' great love for us. Ask them to look at the cross on the page and remind them that Jesus loved us so much that he died on the cross and rose from the dead to a new and glorious life. Explain that it is through the power of Jesus' love that our sins are forgiven and we are reunited with God and others in love. Pause for a moment and invite the children to thank Jesus for loving us so much.
>
> • Read the page with the children. Invite them to fill in the word in the heart. Ask them to compare this heart with the one on page 27 and to explain why they are different. (When we sin, we separate ourselves from God and others. When our sins are forgiven, we are all united again in God's love.)
>
> • Finally, ask them to remember what happened when the shepherd found his lost sheep. (He had a celebration!) Help them see that having our sins forgiven in the Sacrament of Reconciliation is a time to celebrate, too!

Missing word: me.
Activity: Color "THE SACRAMENT OF RECONCILIATION" and the cross.

PAGE 30: Preparing to celebrate the Sacrament of Reconciliation means taking an honest look at our lives — our relationships, our values, and our actions. Under the guidance of the Holy Spirit, we bring to mind the times we have failed to respond to the call to love, we express sorrow for our sins, and we commit ourselves to change. The Rite of Penance (n. 6) tells us that contrition,  "heartfelt sorrow and aversion for the sin committed along with the intention of sinning no more," is the most important act of the penitent.

This page prayerfully guides children in a process of preparing for the sacrament. Parents should be encouraged to use this process with their children at home. The following are some points for catechists and parents to remember:

• Time is not a well-developed concept for children. In examining their lives, children may not be able to remember what they did more than a few days before.

- Help the children focus on one or two things they did wrong on purpose that they are truly sorry for and want to change. Accepting responsibility for what they have done and sincerely wanting to change are the important things.
- If a child is not able to think of anything that he or she did wrong, invite the child to think of how he or she would like to be better.
- The time spent getting ready for the sacrament should be a prayerful time, quiet and free from distractions. It should begin with a prayer asking the Holy Spirit to guide our thoughts and end with a prayer expressing sorrow for our sins.

Preparation: Find some quiet instrumental music to play during "Looking at My Life."

LOOKING AT MY LIFE

1. Imagine you are looking at a TV program. It is the story of *your* life. The first part is about you at home. As you see yourself and the people you live with at home, ask yourself these questions:

- Was I like Jesus (at home)?
- Did I love God and others (at home)?
- Did I help others when they needed it (at home)?
- Did I hurt anyone by what I said or did (at home)?
- Did I think about God and remember to pray (at home)?

Think about your answers. If there was a time when you didn't show love for God and others, try to figure out *why* this happened and *how* you could be better.

2. The second part of the program is about you at school. (Use the same technique as at home.)

3. The third part of the program is about you after school. (Use the same technique as at home.)

4. The last part of the program is about you playing with your brothers or sisters or friends. (Use the same technique as at home.)

5. Now the program is over, and it's time to talk with God. Thank God for the times you saw yourself showing love for him and other people. Tell him you're sorry for the times you were not loving and kind to others. Tell him you want to be better and will try hard to be more like Jesus from now on. Ask God to help you, and thank him for his love and mercy.

- Explain to the children that before we celebrate the Sacrament of Reconciliation we need to take some time to think about our sins — the things we did wrong on purpose. Ask them why this is important. Lead them to see that it can help us understand ourselves better and help us see the ways we need to change.
- Read the first sentence at the top of the page with the children. Invite them to think about where in their home they could find a quiet place to think and pray.
- Read the second sentence and explain that the Holy Spirit will help guide our thoughts so that we will know how we have sinned and how we can be better.

• Call the children's attention to the words to the left of the box. Explain that when we try to think of our sins, sometimes it helps to think about the different parts of our lives — our life with our family at home; our life with the teachers, children, and other people at school; our life with children and others after school; and our life when we play. (Remember that when school is over, many children spend the time in after-school care.)

• Invite the children to read the questions in the box. Tell them that these questions will help them remember what they did or did not do.

• Explain to them that after we think about our sins, we tell God we are sorry and we make up our mind not to sin again. We can do this by praying the Act of Contrition (page 25) or by making up our own prayer. Read the sentences at the bottom of the page and help the children complete them.

• After you have discussed this page with the children, lead them in examining their lives. Ask them to close their eyes and quiet their bodies. Play some soft music and begin with a prayer asking the Holy Spirit to guide the thoughts of the children as they prepare for the Sacrament of Reconciliation. Read "Looking at My Life" (page 63) slowly and reflectively.

Missing words: sorry, better.

SECTION 6: PAGES 31–39 INTRODUCE CHILDREN TO A COMMUNAL CELEBRATION OF THE SACRAMENT OF RECONCILIATION WITH INDIVIDUAL CONFESSION AND ABSOLUTION. *

PAGES 31–33: The communal celebration of the Sacrament of Reconciliation is a powerful sign that we are not alone in our sin and our need for mercy. Nor are we alone in our struggle to overcome sin. The priest mediates our prayerful encounter with God in the Sacrament of Reconciliation. He reflects God's own love for us as he welcomes us and helps us deal with the sin in our lives. As God's representative through ordination, the priest and his words of absolution bring us God's forgiveness and reconciliation. As a representative of the Church — one of us — he reunites us with the community and leads us in praise of God's mercy.

Children can sometimes be apprehensive about the Sacrament of Reconciliation. In the communal celebration, they will have the support of others — their parents and/or catechists, other children, and sometimes other parishioners. Parents and catechists are encouraged to be as positive as possible about celebrating the sacrament. Any negative experiences they may have had should not be passed on. Children should be encouraged to talk about their concerns and assured that the priest is there to help us.

Preparation for page 31: Find out the details of the first celebration of the sacrament, including the name of the priest (or priests) who will hear the children's confessions so that you can refer to him below. If possible, arrange for the priest to drop by for a casual visit with the children.

Find a song related to the Sacrament of Reconciliation such as *Peace Is Flowing Like a River* (Carey Landry) to play while the children are coloring.

* If the children will be celebrating the Sacrament of Reconciliation individually, you may wish to omit pages 32 and 33.

Preparation for page 32: Bring a Bible marked with the parable of the Lost Sheep (Luke 15:4-7). Enthrone it on a table with a cloth and a candle.

- **PAGE 31:** Look at the picture with the children. Explain that when we celebrate the Sacrament of Reconciliation, everyone will gather together in the church — as we do for Mass. Tell them the day, time, and other details of their first celebration of the sacrament. If possible, tell them the name of the priest (or priests) who will lead the celebration.
- Assure them that the priest will be glad to see everyone. Tell them that he loves us and wants to help us, just as Jesus himself would help us.
- Read the page with the children and invite them to color it.

- **PAGE 32:** Look at the picture at the top of the page with the children and explain that we begin as we do at Mass by singing and praying together. If you know the gathering song that will be used, you may want to sing it with them.
- Call the children's attention to the picture at the bottom of the page. Tell them that the next part of the celebration is also like the Mass — we listen to readings from the Bible. Remind them that we should always pay close attention to the readings and the priest's homily because God speaks to us through them.
- Gather the children around the Bible. Proclaim the passage from the Gospel of Luke about the lost sheep. Begin by saying, "A reading from the holy Gospel according to Luke," and end with "The Gospel of the Lord." Invite the children to respond as they would at Mass.
- Ask the children to imagine that they are going to give the homily after the reading. What would they say to the people about the meaning of the Gospel?
- Read the page with the children. Invite them to fill in the missing words and complete the heart. Ask them how they think God's words "change our hearts."

- **PAGE 33:** Look at the picture at the top of the page with the children. Explain that after the homily the priest or another minister helps us examine our lives so that we will know how we have sinned. Then we pray together for forgiveness.
- Read the page with the children and help them fill in the missing words. Explain that when we offer others a sign of peace it is like forgiving them and being forgiven by them. Invite them to draw a picture of themselves offering a sign of peace to the people around them.

Activity on page 31: Color the page.
Missing words on page 32: singing, praying, Bible, sheep.
Activity on page 32: Complete the heart.
Missing words on page 33: Our Father, peace, tell.
Activity on page 33: Draw a picture offering a sign of peace to others.

PAGES 34-37: When we confess our sins to the priest, we enter into a prayerful dialogue with him. In this dialogue, we confront the reality of sin in our lives and allow ourselves to be changed by God's grace. The priest, acting in the place of Christ, accepts our contrition, offers us spiritual advice, and gives us a penance. By accepting the penance, we strengthen our resolve to "sin no more." The priest's words of absolution, often accompanied by a touch on the head or the shoulder, are healing words that bring us inner peace and lead us to praise God for his mercy.

These pages help the children understand what to expect when they confess their sins to the priest. Role-playing the rite is a good way to help children feel more comfortable when they approach the priest. If a reconciliation room will be used, the children should visit it beforehand. As you work through the material with the children, look at the pictures first and then read the sentences. Encourage them to ask questions and to share their concerns.

• **PICTURE 1 (PAGE 34):** Ask the children what they think the priest will say when we come to him. Invite them to write his greeting in the "bubble."

• Compare the priest to the shepherd who found his lost sheep. Remind them that he wants to help us come closer to God. He is not there to scold or punish anyone. Invite the children to fill in the missing word in the sentence at the bottom of the page.

Activity: Write the priest's greeting.
Missing word: sheep.

• **PICTURE 2 (PAGE 35):** Tell the children that the priest will help them begin and that he will guide them throughout the celebration.

• **PICTURE 3 (PAGE 35):** Explain that when we confess our sins to the priest we tell him what we did wrong as best we can and answer any questions he may ask. Invite the children to complete the child's sentence.

• Assure the children that the priest will *never* repeat anything we tell him. Tell them that he is more concerned about helping us know how much God loves us and helping us learn to love him in return than he is about remembering what we did.

Activity: Complete the sentence with what the child in the picture tells the priest.

• **PICTURE 4 (PAGE 36):** Tell the children that after we confess our sins to the priest, he often talks with us. Sometimes he helps us understand how we can change our behavior and encourages us to be better. Invite the children to complete the child's sentence.

Activity: Complete the sentence with how the child in the picture is going to change.

- **PICTURE 5 (PAGE 36):** Explain to the children that the priest sometimes tells us to say some prayers as a penance, or he may tell us to do something connected with what we did. For example, if we were mean to a younger sister, the priest might ask us to play one of her favorite games with her as a penance. Invite the children to complete the priest's sentence.
- Help the children understand that when we accept the penance the priest gives us, we show that we really want to change.

Activity: Complete the sentence with a penance for the child in the picture.

- **PICTURE 6 (PAGE 37):** Explain to the children that when the priest says the prayer of absolution, our sins are taken away and our friendship with God and the people in God's family is made strong again. Tell them that the word "absolve" means *to take away.* Invite the children to write in the child's response.
- Ask the children to notice the position of the priest's hands in the picture. Explain that when the priest forgives our sins he holds his hands over our head, or he may touch our head, as a sign that God loves and forgives us.
- Call the children's attention to the figure of Jesus in the picture. Ask them why they think Jesus is there. Remind them that it is because of Jesus' great love for us that our sins are forgiven.

Activity: Write the child's response to the priest (Amen).

PAGES 38 AND 39: The illustrations and words on these pages lead the children to anticipate the joy of having their sins forgiven and being friends again with God and the community.

Preparation: Find a lively song such as "Joy, Joy, Joy" (Carey Landry) or "Mercy Is Falling" (David Ruis) to sing with the children.

- **PAGE 38:** Recall the story of Zacchaeus with the children and ask them how they think Zacchaeus felt when Jesus forgave him. Ask them how they think the sheep felt when the good shepherd found it. Ask them how they felt when someone forgave them for doing something wrong. Tell them that knowing that God has forgiven our sins in the Sacrament of Reconciliation can give us a feeling of great joy.
- Read the page with the children and invite them to draw a line from the phrase on the left side to the correct phrase on the right side. Read the completed sentences.

- **PAGE 39** is an expression of the warmth and sheer joy we may experience at being loved by God in forgiveness.* Read it with the children and invite them to color both pages.
- Conclude the session by singing one of the songs suggested above with the children.

Completed sentences on page 38: Jesus' love for us has taken away all our sins. We are all together again in peace and friendship. We praise and thank God for his mercy.

Activity on pages 38 and 39: Color the pages.

* The words "hugged by God" are those of Miss Mary Jo Tully, who kindly consented to their use in *Making Things Right.*

PAGES 40-46, THE CONCLUDING PAGES, HELP CHILDREN UNDERSTAND THE CONTINUING JOURNEY OF CONVERSION AND HIGHLIGHT THE IMPORTANCE OF THE SACRAMENT OF RECONCILIATION FOR OUR WHOLE LIFE. THEY SHOULD BE USED AFTER THE CELEBRATION.

PAGES 40 AND 41: Like the Sacrament of Baptism, the Sacrament of Reconciliation marks a new beginning in our lives. It is an opportunity to leave the past behind and start again, forgiven and renewed in God's love. Because of the strong focus on preparing for the sacrament, there is a danger that children will think of the celebration as an end rather than a beginning. These pages lead them to understand that the time after the celebration of the sacrament is an important time for changing and growing stronger in our love for God and others.

Preparation: Provide drawing materials for the children.

> • **PAGE 40:** Talk with the children about their experiences of celebrating the Sacrament of Reconciliation. Ask them to draw a picture of how they felt after their sins were forgiven. Invite them to share their pictures.
> • Help the children understand that the Sacrament of Reconciliation gives us a fresh start.
> • The things we did wrong are gone, and God gives us new strength to grow in love for him and for one another.
> • Explain that growing in love sometimes means that we need to change — for example, from telling lies to telling the truth, from disobeying our parents to doing what they tell us, from saying mean things to others to saying nice things to them, from forgetting about God to thinking about him and praying to him. Ask the children to think about how they would like to change or how they would like to be better. Invite them to close their eyes and say a little prayer asking God to help them stay away from sin and grow in his love.
> • Look at the picture with the children and compare it to the one on page 16. Talk with them about what they see happening. Help them write what the children are saying to one another.
> • Read the page with the children and help them fill in the blanks.
>
> • **PAGE 41:** Call the children's attention to the message at the top of the page and help them decode it.
> • Talk with them about the picture and invite them to tell about times they have seen other children being kind and helpful. Ask them to think of ways that they can follow Jesus. Encourage them to be specific.
> • Read the Scripture passage with the children. Tell them that these are Jesus' words and talk about what he meant by them. Encourage them to remember and keep Jesus' words in their hearts to help them grow in love and care for others.
> • Read the question at the bottom of the page with them. Invite them to think about it and to write down what they will do to be like Jesus. If time permits, have the children share what they wrote.

Activity on page 40: Write what the children are saying to one another.

Missing words on page 40: kindness, grow.

Activities on page 41: Decode the words: follow Jesus. Answer the question at the bottom of the page.

NOTES

PAGES 42 AND 43: Growing in love is a lifelong process with many ups and downs. These pages help children come to an awareness of this process and reemphasize God's deep and abiding love for us.

Preparation: Provide small papers for each child.

• **PAGE 42:** Read the sentences at the top of the page with the children.

• Help them understand that trying to grow in love is similar to trying to learn something new, such as riding a bicycle or playing a musical instrument. Talk with them about the time and effort it takes, and how sometimes even though we try hard, we don't do it right — and sometimes we get tired and want to give up. Explain that learning to love God and others is like that. It takes time, effort, and lots of practice — and we never give up!

• Look at the picture with the children. Invite them to imagine what happened and what the little girl is saying. Help them write her words in the "bubble."

• Read the sentence below the picture with the children. Let them know that we all fail from time to time — and that sometimes even grown-ups fail. If you can share something that you have been trying to work on in your own life and why you keep trying, it will help them understand that they are not alone.

• Help the children understand that prayer is an important part of growing in love. Encourage them to turn to God for the strength they need to do the right thing and assure them that God is always there to help them.

• Give each of the children a small paper and ask them to write how they would like God to help them — for example, "Help me obey my mother," "Help me stop fighting," or "Help me share my toys." When they are finished, gather in a prayer circle and invite each child to read from his or her paper. After each petition, say this response together: "God our Father, hear our prayer."

• **PAGE 43:** Read the sentence at the top of the page with the children. Remind them that God's love doesn't depend on whether we are good or not. God loves us so much that he is always ready to forgive us when we are sorry for what we have done and want to be friends again.

• Invite the children to complete the picture by connecting the dots. Ask them why the parable of the Lost Sheep is a good story for us to remember when we do something wrong. (It tells us how much God loves us and wants us to be near him.)

• Help the children discover the message at the bottom of the page. (Read the words in the parentheses from left to right.)

• If time permits, read *Mama, Do You Love Me?* by Barbara M. Joose (Scholastic) to remind them once again how much God loves us.

Activity on page 42: Write what one child is saying to the other.

Activities on page 43: Connect the dots. Fill in the blanks: Nothing, not even our sins.

69

PAGES 44 AND 45: These pages help children understand that we are encouraged to celebrate the Sacrament of Reconciliation throughout our lives — for the forgiveness of sins, for reconciliation, and to help us deepen our love for God.

> • **PAGE 44:** Look at the picture on the page with the children and ask them how old they think the young people are, beginning with the boy on the left. Talk with the children about growing up. Ask them what they would like to be when they grow up. Ask them if they think they will need to celebrate the Sacrament of Reconciliation when they grow up.
>
> • Help the children understand that as they grow older they will outgrow their clothes, but they will never outgrow their need for the Sacrament of Reconciliation. Tell them there are always times in our lives when we need to be forgiven for what we have done — times when we need God's love and his grace to bring us back home and to help us follow the example of Jesus.
>
> • Read the sentences with the children. Help them fill in the blanks.
>
> • **PAGE 45:** Remind the children that the Sacrament of Reconciliation is a special gift that God has given us to help our love for him and others grow stronger and stronger.
>
> • Tell them that each year during Advent and Lent the people in God's family are reminded to turn to God and to ask for his forgiveness in the Sacrament of Reconciliation. Encourage them to participate in these celebrations of the sacrament with the rest of God's family so that they will continue to grow strong in their love for God and one another. (You may also want to tell them the other times when the sacrament is available — and that it is always available by calling the parish for an appointment.)
>
> • Read the page with the children and help them fill in the missing words.
>
> • Invite them to thank and praise God for his goodness and mercy.

Missing words on page 44: old, love.
Missing words on page 45: peace, love.
Activity on page 45: Color "THANK YOU, GOD!"

PAGE 46: The last page in the book is related to the first page. Sin separates us from others; forgiveness and reconciliation reunite us in love.

> • Look at the picture with the children and invite them to compare it to the picture on the first page of *Making Things Right*. Ask them why they think the girl isn't sitting by herself now.
>
> • Help them to see that "making things right" changes things. When we say we're sorry to the person or persons we hurt, when we try to make up for what we've done, when we really try to be better, we are close to God and each other again — and that makes us feel good all over!
>
> • Conclude the session by singing a joyful song with the children.